Following the Law

If...Then

Sloane Gould

COMPUTER KIDS
Powered by Computational Thinking

Published in 2018 by The Rosen Publishing Group, Inc.
29 East 21st Street, New York, NY 10010

Book Design: Jennifer Ryder-Talbot
Editor: Caitie McAneney

Photo Credits: Cover sergign/Shutterstock.com; p. 4 sirtravelalot/
Shutterstock.com; p. 6 Soloviova Liudmyla/Shutterstock.com; p. 8 John Roman Images/
Shutterstock.com; p. 10-11 Ivan Kokoulin/Shutterstock.com; p. 12 George Rudy/
Shutterstock.com; p. 13 Hata Studio/Shutterstock.com; p. 14-15 TinnaPong/
Shutterstock.com; p. 15 (recycle icon) onair/Shutterstock.com; p. 16-17 Monkey Business
Images/Shutterstock.com; p. 18 LStockStudio/Shutterstock.com; p. 20 CREATISTA/
Shutterstock.com.

Library of Congress Cataloging-in-Publication Data

Names: Gould, Sloane.
Title: Following the law: if...then / Sloane Gould.
Description: New York : Rosen Classroom, 2018. | Series: Computer Kids: Powered by
Computational Thinking | Includes glossary and index.
Identifiers: LCCN ISBN 9781508137733 (pbk.) | ISBN 9781538323977 (library bound) |
ISBN 9781538355404 (6pack) | ISBN 9781538352762 (ebook)
Subjects: LCSH: Law--Juvenile literature. | Law--United States--Juvenile literature. |
Legislation--United States--Juvenile literature.
Classification: LCC K240.G68 2018 | DDC 340--dc23

Manufactured in the United States of America

CPSIA Compliance Information: Batch #WS18RC: For Further Information contact Rosen Publishing, New York, New York at 1-800-237-9932

Table of Contents

Judges interpret the law and look at evidence. They control trials within their courtroom and make important decisions.

What Are Laws?

Laws are rules that people in a community, state, or country must follow. These rules are created to make sure people behave in a way that's safe for themselves and others.

Can you think of some laws that affect you every day? There are many! For example, you must wear a seat belt while you're in a moving car. You must not shoplift, or steal goods from a store. These laws keep you safe and ensure that you act in a respectful way towards others. If you follow laws, then you are a good citizen. If you don't follow laws, then you may be punished.

Different Kinds of Laws

There are many different laws that affect you. It's important to learn about the law. If you know about laws, then you can take steps to follow them.

Some laws are made at the federal level. **Legislators** make laws that affect everyone living in the United States. There are laws about businesses, drugs, health, food **regulations**, and education. There are laws that are made to keep the country safe from pollution and laws about **immigration**. Laws exist on the state level, too. States make laws that only affect people within that state. Local laws affect only people within a certain community.

Local laws decide community-related rules. For example, your community may have a rule about where and when you can build a bonfire.

It is the job of police officers to **enforce** laws.
If a police officer sees someone break the law,
then they have to stop them.

Following the Law

If you educate yourself about laws, then you can follow them. Most laws boil down to treating others with respect and doing your best to keep yourself and others safe.

If you follow the law, then chances are you won't be punished for something. Have you ever heard the phrase: "That will go on your permanent record"? Everyone has a record of the laws that they've broken and how they've been charged for those **offenses**. Following the law keeps your record clean from any charges. That makes it easier to get a good job in the future.

Breaking the Law

If you knowingly break a law, then you may get in trouble for it. If breaking the law hurt someone or put them in danger, then it is often treated as a serious crime.

Police can arrest you for breaking the law. However, you are not charged with a crime until after a trial.

If an adult breaks the law, then they may have to pay a fine or go to jail. It depends on the **severity** of the case. If a young person breaks the law, then they may receive punishment as well. If their action was a mistake, then they might just get a warning. If the action caused great harm, then they might be sent to a **detention center** for young people.

If people break copyright laws, then the creator of the work may lose money.

Copyright Laws

Imagine you just created something that you're very proud of. Maybe you wrote a great poem or song. Maybe you painted a picture or took a photograph. If you create something, then the law says you own its copyright.

Copyright protects your right to do what you want with your work. You can make and sell copies of your own work. If you make or sell copies of another person's work without permission, then you are breaking the law. For example, if you use or share a band's song without their permission, then you are breaking copyright laws.

copyright symbol

©

Littering Laws

Have you ever noticed litter on a street or at the park? Some people throw waste, such as bottles and cans, on the ground. This can harm nature and make communities look dirty. It costs money for the government to clean up litter. Some states have **penalties** for littering.

Check your local laws about littering. If you litter in certain places, then you might get a fine. In some states, leaving a large amount of trash might be considered a felony, or a more serious crime. If you litter again, then the fine might be much more expensive.

If you throw your waste away in the proper way, then you won't get a fine for littering.

Laws for the Road

How can you keep yourself and others safe in a car? You can start with a seat belt. It's the law! If you don't wear a seat belt, then a police officer can give the driver of the car a ticket.

Texting while driving is a danger to yourself and others on the road.

There are many rules for drivers. If someone drives faster than the speed limit, then a police officer can write them a ticket. If someone uses their cell phone while driving, then they may get a ticket. Laws about cell phones differ by state. If someone drives while affected by drugs, then they may even go to jail.

If you act with kindness and respect in school, then you are being a good citizen.

Laws in School

There are laws that affect students every day. In most states, kids between the ages of 6 and 16 have to go to school. If they don't go to school, then it's called truancy. If a student is sick or there is an emergency, then that counts as an excused absence. However, if there are too many unexcused absences, then a parent might have to appear in court.

If a student **harasses** or seriously bullies another student, then the school might punish them. They could be kicked out of their school or unable to attend for a set number of days.

Laws Against Violence

Laws are meant to keep us safe. If people harm others, then we cannot be safe. Therefore, there are many laws against **violence** and harassment.

It is against the law to abuse someone, or treat them with violence. If someone abuses children, animals, or the **elderly**, then they will be punished. If someone harms their **spouse**, coworker, or even a stranger, then they will also be punished. It is up to judges to decide what kind of punishment someone will get for an act of violence. It depends on the severity of the case.

Violence is never the answer. If you disagree with someone, then you can try to talk it out.

What If?

Most people are law-following citizens. They follow the rules of their country, state, and community. If they follow the rules, then they are able to enjoy a clean record and freedom.

What if you do something wrong? If it's a mistake, then you may get away with a warning. If you break a law on purpose, then you may get a penalty. One way to practice being a law-following citizen is to follow the rules in school. If your classroom has a rule against bullying, then don't bully others. Following the law is the easiest way to stay out of trouble!

Glossary

detention center: A place where people who have committed crimes are kept as punishment.

elderly: Someone who is rather old.

enforce: To make sure people obey the law.

harass: To annoy or bother someone repeatedly.

immigration: The process by which people come to a new country to live.

legislator: One who makes laws, especially for a political unit.

offense: The act of breaking the law.

penalty: A punishment for breaking a rule or law.

regulation: A rule or order telling how something is to be done.

severity: Having to do with the level of pain or harm something has caused.

spouse: Someone to whom one is married.

violence: The use of physical force to injure or harm someone.

Index